Ferrets and Ferreting

FERRETS and FERRETING

Iain Brodie

BLANDFORD PRESS

POOLE · DORSET

First published 1978

Copyright © 1978 Blandford Press Ltd,
Link House, West Street,
Poole, Dorset, BH15 1LL

ISBN 0 7137 0903 0

Set in 11/13 pt Baskerville and
Printed in Great Britain by Unwin Brothers Limited,
Woking.
Bound by Robert Hartnoll, Bodmin

Contents

Acknowledgements

I would particularly like to acknowledge the help of Miss Edna Prentice, and Miss Sue Baillie, the two ladies who undertook the typing and correction of the very many spelling and grammatical errors. Also my wife who does not so much nag as nudge when I get behind on schedules—thank you Bev!

I would also like to acknowledge the help of Robin Fletcher who took most of the photographs for the book, and I wish to thank Mrs J. S. Hughes and Miss Patricia Barrell for allowing us to use their ferrets as 'photographic models' the scraper board illustration on the title page was specially prepared by Michael Clark.

IB

Introduction

The object of this book is twofold. It is meant to provide a background to the history of ferreting and the origin of the Ferret. It is also intended to make available information on the Ferret, its housing, feeding, management and breeding, and with an introduction to the uses of the Ferret, particularly for Rabbit hunting.

There is a great deal of folk lore surrounding Ferrets, some of which is more than a little bizarre, some downright stupid and cruel; it also involves a lot of leg pulling. Here, as elsewhere in the book, the opinions expressed are entirely my own,

My intention in writing this book is quite simply to present an introduction to the Ferret and some of its ways. As with all 'arts' —and ferreting can be an art as practised by some—the reader will develop further interest or not as time goes by. What I have set out to do is to provide some ground rules concerning Ferrets; some advice more on what not to do than what to do. While I hope the book will be used as an aid or guide, potential ferreters would do a lot worse than persuading a gamekeeper to give practical instruction in field craft, working a warren, and so forth. It is perfectly possible to write a great deal on what to look for and what to do, but no matter how descriptive the written word, there is no substitute for the maxim 'seeing is believing'. Thus, this book is only a preparation for the time you first take your Ferret out to work, if that is indeed what you decide to do.

Iain Brodie
Summer, 1978

[1]
Origins of Ferrets

Much has been said and written on this topic, and in the absence of any conclusive historical evidence, the origins will probably remain debatable for a long time to come.

However, interpretation of the available information does produce varying opinions, and these are all I can offer here. Certain things can be said with little fear of contradiction, and these are basically that ferreting as a pursuit started most certainly in Continental Europe, and probably in southern or south-eastern Europe. It is most assuredly an extremely ancient pursuit, at the very least 2000 years old.

Moving from certainty to conjecture, it is likely ferreting was practised in the eastern Mediterranean during the Roman Empire. Did it start there? It may have, but I think it started earlier and spread there with the contacts made possible by the expanding Roman influence. Where did it spread from? I personally believe from somewhere in the vicinity of the Black Sea, an area where several early civilisations originated.

Ancestors

Within Europe there are only three possible ancestors, and all are members of the Mustelid family, as is the Ferret. We can dismiss one right away—the Marbled Polecat; the physique of the animal and his skeleton, particularly the shape and size of his skull, rules him out definitely. The other two are very closely related and where their distributions overlap, they can and do hybridise. These candidates are the European Polecat or Foulmart(en) and the Asiatic Polecat or Steppe Polecat. Both animals are nearly identical in size and conformation; they do, however, prefer slightly different habitats and differ in one very fundamental factor, their fur colouring. In the European animal, this is virtually black with an intense white underfur. In contrast, the Steppe Polecat is basically yellowish on the body with a darker belly and, most importantly, it has an off-white or nicotine coloured under-fur. Personally, I believe the under-fur colouring is significant in identifying both the ancestor of the Ferret and through this, the area in which ferreting originated.

It is also interesting to note that if you cross a Steppe Polecat or a Ferret with a European Polecat, you will always, in the first cross, produce an animal with a nicotine coloured under-fur. This is also the case even if you repeat it a second and third time. Unless you have a tame European Polecat with which to make a direct comparison, it is very easy to believe the under fur of your animal is white and therefore European. It most certainly will not be so.

There are a number of other good reasons for thinking that the Steppe Polecat was the original basic material.

In experiments conducted by Dr. Trevor Poole at the University of Aberystwyth in Wales, European Polecats were crossed in both directions with Ferrets. In the behaviour of the youngsters, it was found that a lot of the behaviour of the European parent was transmitted to the offspring, and this included a lot of aggression and different reactions to being handled. It is obviously quite pointless going ferreting with an animal whose reactions are unpredictable and which is liable to perform digital surgery on your hands whenever it is in the mood. Certainly, it does not lead to lasting and trustful *rapport* between man and beast.

Taming and Domestication

A further fundamental point to consider is that any animal or bird can be tamed after a fashion. Each species has its 'characters', some of whom will be easier to deal with, while some other litter mates will be much harder. This taming can be done in just one generation, but it is a world away from domestication. Taming and domesticating are not, and never have been the same thing. It takes many hundreds of years, even thousands, to domesticate any new species. Taming a wild animal is merely one step down a very long road to domestication, and on the way you often alter (in different ways) the animal's body and more easily, by inbreeding or selective breeding, its coat colour. The Ferret's coat colour is different in many respects from the European Polecat's, including its high incidence of albinism. Albinos are extremely rare in nature and only become common by man's interference. History tells us that either by accident or design, Ferrets mated with wild European Polecats in the British Isles and elsewhere. Yet this did not and could not alter the basic Ferret, which had most probably evolved over 2000–3000 years, and possibly even longer than that.

The Ferret has only in recent times in Western Europe been used to hunt Rabbits and Rats, neither of which were to be found in the British Isles before the time of the Roman occupation.

Original Use

Originally, the Ferret was used on rodents such as European Sousliks, Steppe Marmots and Hamsters. The Rabbit originated in the Western Mediterranean, spreading from Spain through France and Germany. It was also introduced to mainland Britain, then Ireland, as a delicacy, but soon showed its potential! Before long, every estate and village had their well managed warrens. At that time it was known as the Coney, while the juveniles were known as Rabbits; later, common useage left the adult being known as Rabbit and the young as Kits. From England it was taken to Ireland and then during the 18th century finally made its appearance in Scotland, where it is known in Gaelic as *coineach*. In German the Rabbit is known as *Kaninchen* and in

Albino Ferret: these animals have pink eyes and an absence of skin pigmentation. Normally this is rare among wild animals.

French *lapin* (*de Garenne*). The Polecat in German is known as *Iltis* and in French as *putois*.

The Sousliks and Marmots especially are found in colonies much like Rabbit warrens. The adult Rabbit weighs around 2kg or 5lbs, the Sousliks about 300g or 12oz on average, while the Marmot is a very worthwhile 4–8kg or 9–17lb. Just think how long one of those would feed a family compared with a Rabbit. Except for the youngsters, however, they are very much out of a bitch Ferret's league as 'prey', but using a dog Ferret and nets the result would be the same, one in—everybody out! Working with a dog would probably be very productive. Did I say a dog? You most probably would need a pack to round up that lot while the Ferret played ghosties downstairs.

Conclusions

The evidence, factual and circumstantial, leans very heavily in favour of the Steppe Polecat being the original ancestor of today's Ferret, and whoever brought the Rabbit to the British Isles fairly certainly did it as a means of a future food supply and not because they 'just liked bunnies'. They must also have brought the means to kill them—in the form of ready trained hunters. These people would certainly have also brought their Ferrets. Apart from occasional infusion of wild blood from British versions of European Polecats (as explained before), the Ferret is quite definitely an immigrant and not of native stock.

[2]
Ferreting—Past and Present

Ferreting is alive and well, as both a pastime and as part and parcel of full-time trapping by hunters, gamekeepers and pest controllers.

Advocates and practitioners range from schoolboys to seasoned veterans of the rural arts, all with their pet methods and theories which, while working well for them, have just as many detractors.

Rabbits

In times past, the margin between a full stomach for all the family and hunger was a very narrow one; if a food resource failed partly or in total, without leaving an alternative, then disaster loomed large and real. It was important for families, several co-operating families or villages to be able to turn to alternative food sources by harvesting nature's surplus; and this surplus included the Rabbit. It has generally been considered that the Rabbit spread along the Mediterranean from the Iberian Peninsular, progressing north through Europe and then being taken to the British Isles either by the Romans or the Normans. Recently, however, information produced by an English University could make this theory completely obsolete. From reputed fossil bones, it is now being suggested that the Rabbit was in fact in the British Isles long before the Norsemen raided and then settled the coasts of France, before moving on to invade England in 1066. In fact, it is now likely that Rabbits were to be found in southern England before the Roman Empire was even a remote thought among the tribes of the Italian Peninsula. Could Rabbits have crossed the land bridge with Europe before the English Channel broke through?

Where you find one Rabbit you are most likely to find a lot more—it is in the nature of the beast. The original theory was that they were brought over to the British Isles and established in warrens under controlled conditions. The new theory would suggest that owing to an unaltered (or barely so) predator population, Rabbits numbers were kept at a level which must have been low, and so to compensate for times of famine some of them were caught up and confined in artificial warrens. Whichever theory is the case, it remains a fact that in some parts of Europe, Rabbits were kept in semi-captivity with the specific purpose of providing food for a particular community. In fact, Rabbits were so important in England that it was a crime to hunt them, as they belonged to the owner of the land. However, this was not the case in Scotland. Their arrival in that country is comparatively recent, 300 to 400 years in the south perhaps and 200 years in the north, and they have no legal status at all.

Albino Ferret investigating scent which can be of rabbit, vole or other rodent.

In those areas where the Rabbit had greatest economic significance, central and southern England for example, an entire livelihood, or a large part of it, was provided for one member of the community. Being in charge, that person was called a 'warrener'. In fact, there are still people today with the surnames Warren, Warrener and Warrender, either from their ancestors working at that profession or living in the vicinity of a warren; and place names can be found incorporating the word 'warren'.

The economic importance attached by man to his sporting interests often led to the total extermination of species of birds and animals, who while preying on Rabbits also took gamebirds. Thus, by taking away the natural means of control of Rabbits through eliminating or reducing their predators, Rabbit numbers had to be controlled by other means. Frequently, this was done by using the warrener's favourite tool, the Ferret. In fact the job of modern gamekeepers often evolved from that of warrener, and many most likely have combined both functions for some time.

Parallel to all of this was the activity of individuals with their own Ferrets and who carried out their own hunting. In England this form of hunting was illegal without permission from the landowner. This activity evolved into the noble profession of poacher. Whilst not without its dangers of course, poaching, although illegal, never carried much of a social stigma for those caught in the activity.

Urbanisation and Country Life

For several hundred years the Ferret has been very widely kept and used in rural areas. However, with the coming of the Industrial Revolution, the general movement of country people to the towns naturally included many from gamekeeping families and they took with them their Ferrets and the associated skills in using them. These skills have been passed down to their descendants and amongst their friends and so there are now almost certainly more people keeping Ferrets in urban areas than

Ferret at entrance to burrow, returning to handler, having failed to find anyone at home.

in the countryside. Within the British Isles it is still usually the case that Rabbits are the property of the owner of the land on which they are found, especially in England, where the laws concerning trespass are more clearly defined than in Scotland. There you cannot poach a Rabbit because you can only poach something which belongs to someone else and the Rabbit belongs to no-one. It is, and always will be, wisest to ask the owner if you can work his Rabbits, because if he has a lot he will probably be more than willing to give permission. The Rabbit still can be the cause of large losses to the farmer, especially when they are at the peak of the population cycle. This usually occurs before myxymatosis returns once again, as it always seems to do every few years. Ask first; it is always best and costs nothing but it shows you know that you must fit into the rhythm of the countryside and are not likely to go on the rampage. If you can't fit into the countryside, you make enemies and catch no Rabbits—so what's the point? Obtaining permission is one good way to be sent to all the likeliest places and get the best results.

Rats

Associated with urban areas, derelict or otherwise, is the Rat, an animal of fairly recent arrival in Europe and a creature some people will hunt with Ferrets. Personally, I think it is just about one of the most stupid and totally reckless things one can do, yet people do it and will continue to do it, notwithstanding the very high risk of disease if bitten by Rats, and the strong likelihood of death from such a bite. Indeed, a single nip is quite sufficient, but some people always seem ready to take the gravest of risks in most activities.

[3]
Natural History

It is necessary to look at the Ferrets' wild relatives, the Polecats, in order to achieve a better understanding of the life and requirements of Ferrets in captivity.

Among Ferrets there is quite a variation in size among both males and females; to a certain extent this is due to normal genetic variation, but it is most often caused by either in-breeding and/or improper feeding of youngsters and their mother before the young are weaned.

Inbreeding is a very frequent failing and the existence of albino specimens best illustrates this. It is, however, often argued that albinos are easier to see when working, which is an interesting explanation since they are chiefly working underground. Would that I had such X-ray vision! Certain attitudes favouring one colour type against another, because of supposed vigour, is patently silly, and those who believe it only fool themselves and mislead others. It is enough to like and prefer certain markings without inventing excuses. There is a very real risk of loss of vigour to be experienced when repeatedly inbreeding your animals, generation after generation. A high risk exists also of ending up with deformed kits in their litters, which is a terrible thing. Among wild Polecats there is little variation in size between members of each sex, although dogs are bigger than bitches. Body lengths are roughly 30–45cm ($12\frac{1}{2}$–$17\frac{1}{2}$in) with the tail 13–19cm (5–7in). The biggest dogs 'weigh up to 1500g (52oz), while bitches weigh about half of this at 800g (30oz).

The immediate impression of a European Polecat, when first seen, is of a black animal with a white face mask and a light coloured belly. The Polecat–Ferret, as the non-albino Ferret is often called, varies a great deal in colouring, usually with a face mask, sometimes rather indistinct, and a yellowish brown fur overall with a yellow belly colour.

Distribution

With the exception of Ireland, the Western Islands of Scotland and northern Scandinavia, the European Polecat was well distributed throughout most of Continental Europe. Its range overlaps with the Asiatic or Steppe Polecat, ancestor of the Ferret, in parts of Hungary, Czechoslovakia and Romania and it is entirely replaced by the Steppe Polecat *Mustela eversmannii* in the Balkans, Bulgaria and the Black Sea areas of the USSR.

However the modern distribution is now sadly altered, with the European Polecat under pressure over much of its range in Western Europe. Generally speaking, it is now only found in low population areas which are often remote hill and mountain terrain. The preferred habitat is open woodland, scrub, and areas of rock and scree. The trees most commonly associated with this terrain are Birch and Alder, also old open Oak and Beech forest which allows plenty of vegetation and undergrowth most favoured by prey species. By the same token, Polecats are least likely to be found in any numbers in large areas of coniferous forest.

In the British Isles they are still absent from Ireland, although Feral Ferrets are sometimes recorded there. Wales remains their stronghold, from where they are slowly spreading into those English counties immediately adjacent to the Welsh border. In the north of England, in the Lake District, a very few managed to survive. In recent years, they have been increasingly helped along by re-introduction of Welsh animals by at least one individual whom I know. Elsewhere in England, it is fair to say that any 'Polecats' to be found are most likely to be Feral Ferrets, both albinos and the Steppe Polecat type.

The situation in Scotland is not at all good, but it has been getting better—mainly due to re-introductions. The last European Polecats in Scotland were (or are) to be found in Sutherland in the far north. In the very early 1900's, their numbers were extremely low and some authorities believed they did, in fact, become extinct. Whether this was the case or not has never been fully resolved. A large and successful population of Ferrets exists in the mountains on the large island of Mull on the west coast. These are very definitely descendants of Ferrets which escaped or were released, and are not European Polecats. Other Ferral Ferret populations exist elsewhere in Scotland, both on the mainland and the islands. Some survive well enough, some come and go depending on whether someone working Ferrets looses a few animals or not.

Re-introductions of Polecats of known undiluted ancestry have been successfully made in two areas of the West Highland coastline, and an area on, or near, Loch Ness. These animals appear to be surviving and extending their ranges. The question of re-introducing any species is fraught with many problems, the most important of which is the need to be 110% certain that the animals are pure bred from wild stock. It is highly reprehensible to release Ferrets which are thought to look like Polecats—very few people have any idea what a real live Polecat looks like, let alone having ever handled one. Comparing Ferrets with Polecats is like comparing alley cats with Wildcats.

The European Polecat is a member of a large family of animals known as Mustelids or Mustelidae, distantly related to the cat family. In size they range from the Weasel, the smallest of which is about 20cm (8in) including tail and weighing 50g ($1\frac{3}{4}$oz) or over; the largest being the Wolverine or Glutton, of which large males can reach over $1 \cdot 10$m (42in) and weigh about 14kg (30lb). Both of these are found in Continental Europe. Other Mustelids found in Europe are Pine Marten, Stone Marten (sometimes known as Beech or Baum Marten) Stoat, Otter, Badger, Steppe Polecat, Marbled Polecat, Least Weasel, European Mink and the introduced American Mink.

The habits of both the European Polecat and the Ferrets' ancestor, the Steppe Polecat, are broadly similar, but differ in one major way. The first animal is often associated with trees and

[15]

scrub, the second is to be found in mainly treeless areas. They both locate food by scent and hearing, their eyesight being of secondary importance. To a certain extent they may well be able to sense vibrations from underground through their footpads. Food includes mice, frogs, ground nesting birds, rabbits young and old; they can swim too, if put to it, so they may well take fish on occasion. The main variation for the Steppe Polecat is in exchanging Rabbits for Hamsters and Sousliks or Ground Squirrels. Both types will take Rats, Shrews, Voles and Moles. Neither farmers nor sportsmen are very fond of either species of Polecat due to their great liking for domestic poultry and game birds. Ferrets also retain this ancestral taste for expensive foods and they are no better thought of for it either!

Polecat dens are to be found under old sheds, barns, hollow trees, old rabbit burrows or fox earths; occasionally, they will dig their own dens, often with several entrances. Bedding may consist of bracken, grasses and sheep's wool usually dragged into the den by walking backwards and pulling it after them.

Most members of the Mustelid family are affected in their breeding cycle by a process known as delayed implantation; two exceptions to this rule are the Polecats and the Mink, both belonging to the *Mustela* genus. They mate in March or April, with Polecats able to produce a second litter later in the summer. The gestation period, from time of mating to birth, is roughly 42 days. The young can number from 2–6, but tend to be 5 or 6 as a rule. They are blind and quite hairless when born, but develop rapidly and are weaned at 8 weeks. They remain as a family group learning their craft, slowly breaking up towards October or November. Usually, the young dogs are first to leave, and as with all Mustelids, they wander quite far and wide looking for territories, but being constantly moved on by resident adult dogs. One of the benefits of this is the reduced likelihood of the in-breeding of closely related animals. Less than half of the male Polecats born in any one year live to see the next spring, and just over a quarter of all females fail to get through their first winter. A three year old Polecat can be said to have done very well for himself in the world, and five year old Polecats are very rare

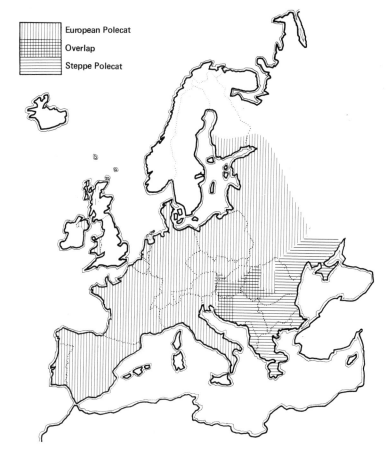

European Polecat
Overlap
Steppe Polecat

Fig. 1 European distribution of Polecat species.

indeed, yet they live for twice that age in captivity.

Occasional hybrids between European Mink and European Polecats have been reported from the USSR, but the product appears to be a mule. The Mink is considered to be an aquatic evolvement from the Polecat.

All Mustelids mark their territory by the use of anal glands. The Polecat is no exception and its smell can be quite strong; this is especially so if the animal has been frightened. In the

[17]

English speaking parts of the British Isles the animal is known as the Foul Mart or Foumart, whereas the Pine Marten is known as the Sweet Mart. This stems from the pungent smell of the dung heaps used as territorial markers, or as latrines outside the den. The animal *itself* does not smell so unpleasant I think in my view, but the stench of its dung is out of this world. The voice of the European and Steppe Polecats and Ferret are, for all practical purposes, the same. It consists of an alarm call which can best be described as a chattering noise, while an aggressive Polecat will often hiss, sounding rather like 'siss' or 'sisiss'.

Polecats and Ferrets are not the best of climbers, nor are they the fastest of runners. They remind me more of a hunched back geriatric Pine Marten as they shuffle around. A quick lunging rush is all they usually manage; but then it is all they really need! They locate the scent of their prey, follow it picking up sounds as they home on to it. Then, having sighted it, they complete the stalk and then pounce in a rush. In turn, Polecats fall to other predators, but usually only when times are hard, such as in mid-

Albino Ferret: a healthy and alert animal, keen and raring to go.

Dog Ferret ready to go down on a line, notice collar and
line knotted at 12 in (30 cm) intervals.

winter. They do not figure highly in any animal's food preferences,
owing to the scent glands and a defence which can be relied upon
to be spirited. However, if you are a hungry and near to starving
Fox, Wildcat or large bird of prey, then you cannot afford to be
very choosy. The worst predator of all, of course, is man, but his
excessive zeal in pursuing the Polecat is past its peak. No doubt
this is due in large measure to there being few Polecats to pursue.
Large, even huge, quantities of pelts from Polecats were sold
through the Fur Auctions at Dumfriess and Inverness in Scotland
for hundreds of years; along with Fox, Marten, Beaver, these
pelts were exported to Europe. When furs became more readily
and cheaply available from North America, trapping as a way of
life virtually died out and the Polecat began to recover. But then
their increased numbers conflicted with gamekeepers' interests
and their total extermination in the British Isles was only just
avoided. On the Continent they were cleared from large areas
and their recovery had to wait for the reduction in the number
of gamekeepers caused by two world wars. It is now unlikely that

the Polecat will be exterminated, and it may even return to much of its old territories.

In some respects, the Steppe Polecat has suffered a worse fate. Large parts of its range have now been brought into cultivation and the plough and animal burrows just do not mix at all well. Without the prey, species that live in the burrows, you cannot have many Polecats. This shows how easy it is to exterminate an animal without even harming a single one of them; one merely has to destroy a habitat.

What is true about the situation of the Steppe Polecat is even worse for the Black-Footed Ferret of North America. This animal lives and hunts in much the same way as the Steppe Polecat, and due to the large scale ploughing up of the prairies and consequent destruction of Prairie Dogs, its main food, this Ferret is now on the Endangered Species List. It only took about 100 years to get there!

[4]
Ferrets for Fur Production

All fur types fall in and out of favour with the dictates of fashion, and the pelt of the Ferret, known in the fur trade as 'fitch', is no exception. Before dealing with this subject in any detail, the reader should firmly fix in his mind some very basic, constant truths. Firstly, fur production is famed, whatever the pelt, for its ability to make and break people financially. For every good year you can expect another year in which to break even and one in which to lose money. There are no quick fortunes and no easy money, part-time or full-time. It can be a good business if carried out efficiently, but there are no short cuts.

Fur of Quality

The next point to bear in mind is that any old bundle of pelts will not be assured of a sale. They must be sorted firstly into males and females, then into matched bundles—matched for colour and matched for quality. All the best quality pelts are obtained in November–December, when the animals are in their first bloom of winter pelt. From then on the quality deteriorates as their fur coats become tattered with wear. Unless you can sell privately, which is most unlikely, sales are achieved through an auction house (such as Hudsons Bay and Annings in London). All pelts are sent to them dried and stretched, they sort and grade and only if you are lucky will your pelts find a bidder under the auctioneer's hammer. The only guidelines on prices are the

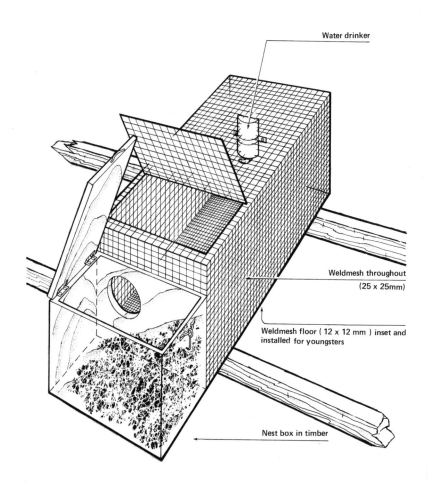

Water drinker

Weldmesh throughout
(25 x 25mm)

Weldmesh floor (12 x 12 mm) inset and
installed for youngsters

Nest box in timber

Fig. 2 Fitch cage for fur production, based on
the type used at most mink farms.

previous sales prices and no one, but no one, can forecast what you will get—don't even try asking.

One of the only ways to achieve good quality pelts is to feed the animals the very best of the freshest food. Second best will not do and there is no point starting unless you accept that fact. It is also very wrong and foolish to even think about fur production unless you have an adequate supply of food all through the year, remembering that a bitch Ferret and her litter, possibly of up to 10 will eat, and eat, and eat. The food *must* be fresh and many problems and losses are a result of food which is decayed.

Housing

Figure 2 will give some idea of type of cage suitable for fur production. It is vital that the floor be of wire, otherwise the droppings build up and foul the pelt and this defeats the whole object. Also, it is unhygienic, which is more important to the Ferret.

An illustration of a type of fur breeding shed most commonly used for Mink is shown in Fig. 3. It is essential to remember that the Ferret was known colloquially as the Foul Marten or Foulmart and not without reason, the droppings smell strongly, and you cannot contemplate keeping a lot of Ferrets in this way in a built-up area. The neighbours will object (quite rightly) and the Public Health Authority will close you down.

Assuming you have none of the above restrictions, the ground upon which the droppings fall is best left as bare earth and must not be concreted over. The reason is that the liquid element of the manure, once it has soaked into the concrete, leaves a strong and permanent smell.

Management

When breeding Ferrets for either their pelts or sale of youngsters, it is only necessary to keep one dog to serve five bitches. When the youngsters have been weaned and the mother removed, it is

[23]

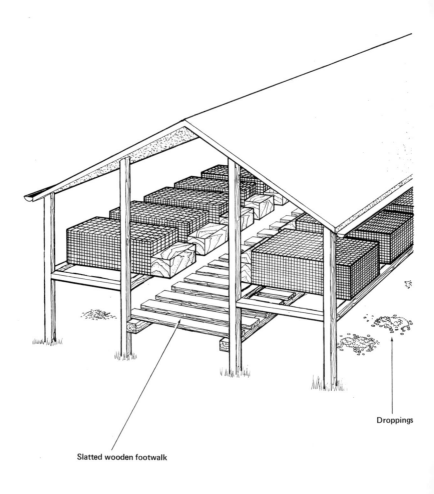

Droppings

Slatted wooden footwalk

Fig. 3 Layout of shed accommodating a number of Fitch units.

necessary as they get older and larger to keep sub-dividing the litters. Firstly divide them by sex to avoid fighting over food and ensuring fair shares for all and keep splitting them up until a maximum of two bitches and one dog are left in each pen.

Continue feeding as much as they can cram each day, clearing away surplus in the evening. The bigger they are, the better will be the pelt in November. Your breeding stock should be on a maintenance diet, however, as animals which are too fat can have difficulty mating and problems at kitting time.

It is well worth bearing in mind that developing good breeding stock takes several years to evolve a 'type', and in comparison with other producers you will have to work up their quality and prices.

With good management, it can and often is possible to get a second litter from most bitches. It does provide a test of your feeding regime to get them into good pelt condition and on time too. Having produced your kitts and having then fed them to the maximum, they should start putting on a very attractive winter coat. There is no point in pelting out too soon, and if things are left too long you lose out in that direction also. Getting your timing right is an art developed over the years and there are no short cuts.

There are several methods of killing out, but the most universally used among mink farmers is carbon dioxide gassing. The best source of information on this could be obtained from the Mink Breeders Association who would have the names of suppliers of the necessary equipment. At the beginning it would be best wherever possible to get the assistance and, ideally, the use of a mink farmer's equipment. This includes tumbler, knives, gassing chamber, drying boards and papers, etc. Having good pelts and wasting them with bad cutting and drying would be quite tragic.

Conclusions

It is always worth remembering that the fur trade is a spender of large sums of money. It is very fussy what it buys and your tatty old skins are of no interest. There is only one position to be in and that is the best. Before pelting time, select your top animals for next season's breeding. Only the best will do; sell the poor specimens live for ferreting, for which they will do well enough, or pelt them. The quality of future years depends on the quality of the breeding stock which you keep. Foundation stock can sometimes be bought from existing fitch farmers, of which there are only a few in Britain.

However, there are many people farming Ferrets in Europe and quite a few large farms particularly in Eastern Europe, especially Poland.

This chapter on breeding Ferrets for fur production is not meant nor intended to be anything other than a sketchy outline of the problems—of which there are many. Anyone thinking of producing Ferrets for their fur will need a great deal of patience and money for a start, and it would be as well to obtain as many of the books, old and new, on Mink ranching. Then seek out the local mink farm for some practical advice.

[5]
Diseases and Illness—Cause, Treatment and Prevention

As with any type of accident, everyone believes it will not happen to them, but you can be fairly sure few people have ever kept any animal without experiencing health problems of one sort or another. As a very rough generalisation, disease is often present as a result of some outside factor, whereas illness is often the result of bad management through carelessness or ignorance, particularly in connection with bad housing and hygiene.

If something goes wrong, do not automatically blame someone else or make excuses. As likely as not, when you think the matter through, something that you did, or more likely did not do, is the probable cause. Everybody, no matter how experienced, will make mistakes and often simple ones at that. But when your Ferret is dead, whether the mistake was a big one or a little one, the result cannot be changed no matter how good your veterinary surgeon.

Illness

Taking illness first, at the risk of sounding hackneyed, the best cure is prevention. Most illness can be avoided altogether by not letting them happen in the first place. Ferrets are pretty hardy little creatures, and if very simple rules are followed, then a lot of problems are solved. All Ferrets need are dry beds, freedom from draughts, clean hutches, clean and proper food.

Dealing with the bedding first, whatever there is, there must be plenty of it—wood shavings, clean straw or hay. Fill the nest box and do not worry about the apparent bulk; it will soon compact down. What is more, Ferrets enjoy burrowing down through the bedding and like being completely hidden, as it gives a feeling of security. This removes a lot of stress, which can often induce illness. Freedom from draughts does not mean necessarily that all sides of kennel or hutch must be enclosed. However, it does mean that apart from a 'pop hole' entrance to the nest box section, this area must be completely enclosed. It is sufficient to have the roof and back completely covered over.

Whatever people might tell you to the contrary, Ferrets are clean animals. It is entirely up to the owners if they stay that way. Only an ill Ferret will foul its bedding; healthy animals always use a latrine, usually in one corner. At the chosen point they reverse into it with upraised tail while either urinating or dropping a scat. These scats vary in colour according to diet, but should be fairly firm, about pencil thickness and 2cm long; if they are a sticky shapeless mass, then your Ferret is not a healthy one. Change its diet as a first priority.

Personally, I believe a wire floor is essential. Ideally, it should be of a strong welded mesh which will allow all of the urine and a lot of the scats to fall right through. This eliminates the risk of a condition known often as 'wet belly', where the underside of the animal hardly has an opportunity to dry off, with very unpleasant consequences and great discomfort. With a wire floor, a weekly scrubbing down will keep the kennel clean and hygienic. To do this, remove your animal to its carrying case or a spare box which is secure, and disinfect everything inside thoroughly to prevent an infestation of mites building up. Prevent, prevent—for it is always easier and cheaper than cure, cure.

Once you have scrubbed it all out, rub an old scat in the corner you want them to use. Use a stick dipped in the scat. This seems like a strange thing to do, but it isn't really. Ferrets are territorial animals and they locate their scats as markers for their 'territory'. This lets other animals know that it is the Ferrets ground and they are in residence—so 'don't come any closer'. They will always renew old scats to keep their own scent fresh, and this is why you should use their habit to get them to use the latrine. This should be best placed for your later cleaning out.

Symptoms that you should always look for are an animal which seems stiff in the way it walks, uneaten food, weepy eyes, the sticky scats I mentioned before, wheezing, coughing, sneezing and constant scratching, especially of the ears. All of these signify an ailing animal. There may not be much wrong with it, but more likely that there is and it is almost always a result of your carelessness. Ear scratching means the Ferret most probably has parasitic mites; this is usually caused by a dirty kennel and dirty bedding. Remedy this immediately or they will seriously affect your Ferret, causing a lot of unnecessary suffering along the way. A Ferret which keeps stopping to scratch itself is more likely to have Rabbits dying from laughter than from the attack of the Ferret. You cannot expect a Rabbit to take your Ferret seriously in such a state! An odd sneeze need not cause too much concern, but if it happens frequently during any period, then beware for the animal has a chill. This is most probably a result of damp bedding and it should be checked immediately.

Diseases

Moving on to diseases proper, there are several which affect the Ferret and all his close relatives. They also affect cats and dogs, who can expose your Ferret, if it is not inoculated, to the disease as carriers, while not necessarily suffering from it themselves. In this category I am thinking mainly of canine distemper (sometimes called by the rather silly name of sweats) and feline enteritis. There is absolutely no reason why any adult Ferret should die from either of these infections, the remedy is simple enough—prevention! Take the animal to the veterinary surgeon and get it inoculated. Why bother rearing, keeping and training what may become a useful member of the family only to have it die as a result of a cat or dog leaving behind its infection while passing through your garden.

Another great leveller of Ferrets is mange which can also be contracted from dogs. Other sources of mange include Rats, either when out working your Ferret on Rats or feeding Rats to them. The latter is not a practice to be entertained or recommended other than by the very most ignorant of fools. To kill Rats is sufficient of a hazard, but to handle them in any way is not only going to expose your Ferret, yourself, your family and possibly the whole neighbourhood to the risk of Weils Disease Plague. There is nothing clever, smart or brave about that; it just proves how hopeless you are at feeding your animal the proper diet of Rabbit, poultry waste or culls.

There are old-time remedies, treatments aplenty about how to treat the above diseases and the majority are totally ineffective as cures, but are highly dangerous to both treater and treated. Just ignore them if anyone ever offers such pearls of wisdom. It is worth bearing in mind that the fur industry has invested huge sums of money in providing cheap and highly effective treatments for Mink and Ferrets, and it is very easy and safe to visit your local vet. Nowadays vets tend not to see so many Ferrets in some areas and could well be quite glad of the chance to practise their highly professional expertise, and such treatment could well turn out to be a lot cheaper in the long run than some of the crazy remedies I have heard.

Very rarely a case of foot rot occurs. If it happens to your Ferret, then two things are obvious—your Ferret's kennel must be indescribably filthy and such neglect suggest that you ought not to be left in charge of even a dead bluebottle fly! This ailment is caused by a fungus which eats away at the pads of the Ferret's feet. There is no cure for other than the very slightest of infection. It is far better to administer a hard and fatal blow to the back of the Ferret's head, bury it decently as a monument to your cruelty, then burn the hutch and forget all about ferreting—for you are just not up to it.

Apart from mange caused by the sarcoptic mite, other parasites to watch for are fleas, ticks and other mites. There are very simple, straightforward and inexpensive methods of getting rid of them and remedies are available either from pet shops or veterinary surgeons. They only require common sense and care in application. It does not always follow that your animals are not properly cared for if you get a 'visitation'. The stage at which

Albino Ferret hunting through spring vegetation.

you will be open to criticism is if they have them for any length of time, as they could be a hazard to humans. This is especially true of mange, which is known as scabies and is as unpleasant as a bed full of nettles. If your Ferret is constantly scratching, which produces both bald patches in the fur and broken patches of skin which look rather raw, then you can be fairly sure it has mange and the sooner it is treated the better for all concerned.

Another source of illness and occasional death is intestinal infection, the first sign of which is noticeable in sticky, shapeless scats. This is due to a much higher than normal quantity of *E. coli* bacteria, originating most frequently from bad food, either stale or over-ripe, and most often associated with feeding animal on poultry offal. It is unusual for this sort of infection to occur in autumn, winter or spring, but it is highly likely in the hot summer months. It can best be avoided by thoroughly cooking the food. Fortunately, as we feed our animals (including several Mustelids, Foxes, Crows, Owls, Birds of Prey and Wildcats) almost entirely on day-old chick culls, we have not to date experienced some of the more unpleasant effects of infected food which all too often is suffered by others; but there is always a first time for everyone, and some day I may get careless. However, it has nothing to do with luck.

Aleutian disease is something of a nightmare for Mink farmers and can cause the loss of a great many animals and cost them their livelihood. The Polecat and his half-brother the Ferret are first cousins of the Mink and so I can see little reason why Ferrets should not contract this disease. However, so far as I know, it has not yet been identified in Ferrets. This does not mean they do not get it, just that no one has spotted it, and with one or two exceptions that I know of, this is mainly due to Ferrets being kept in relatively small numbers, well isolated from Mink farms. Aleutian disease is controllable in Mink and it originates in North American Mink imported by European fur farms. Perhaps the reason why it has not yet been found in Ferrets is that few farmers keep Ferrets for their fur and those who do are not in the market to supply animals as working Ferrets. In terms of price alone, if for no other reason, they can get far more for the animal's pelt than for a live sale. Should Aleutian Disease be contractable by Ferrets, then it will hopefully be contained within fur farms. The moral of this story is keep your Ferrets well away from Mink and do not buy Ferrets from fur farms.

Stockmanship

The best way of ensuring the good health of any animal, be it Pigs, Cattle, Canaries or Ferrets, is good stockmanship and this stems from regular daily contact, handling and observing. This way you know the moment your Ferret is 'off form'; it may not be anything serious, but you will then be on your guard. Perhaps it was slower than usual coming out for its meal, or maybe the eyes seem duller than normal. The best person to treat illness in your Ferrets and other animals is a veterinary surgeon and so if you insist in trying some of the crazy medicaments quoted else-where, then the cost of recifying the damage that is done, assuming the Ferret survives, is potentially astronomical. After you have kept Ferrets for a little while, you will be able to administer minor treatment yourself under the guidance of your veterinary surgeon, treating cuts and bites, delousing and so forth. A good rule is 'what you would not do to yourself, do not do to your poor Ferret'.

Gangrene

Finally, a word of caution. Carnivores, which include the Ferret, contract gangrene extremely quickly. We lost an Arctic Fox bitch during the winter from a neck bite when she was playing the fool with our equally foolish Wolfcub bitch. She went off colour within a day—even overnight—but because of her long fur the bite was not spotted until the second morning. Despite repeatedly cutting out the infected skin and flesh, we had to put her down on the fourth day. The smell of gangrene is quite the most appalling I have ever experienced. Apparently in the initial stages the pain is not intense, just a dull ache, but afterwards the agony is horrific. Always keep a good antiseptic cream with which to treat bite and scratches. If your Ferret gets a skin tear, then have it treated or stitched as required and let your veterinary surgeon be the best judge of that. In the wild the average life-span of most species of male Mustelids is eighteen months; for females it is longer. One of the explanations for such a short life is territorial conflicts; another is predation or fights with other carnivores and hunting accidents. Where this involves bites or torn skin, gangrene is often the cause. Gamekeepers, for instance, often reckon that when you shoot a fox, even if it does not drop dead right away, to prick it with a few pellets is enough—gangrene will do the rest in time.

[6]

Housing and Feeding

There really is little point in intending to keep Ferrets, or any other animals, unless you can provide proper living quarters for them. A sound policy based on simple common sense is to provide the Ferret's hutch before even looking for your Ferret. You have to be absolutely sure that the hutch is properly made, both to keep the Ferret healthy and, equally important, to keep it from escaping. If it is possible to find a way out, you can be sure that your Ferret will find it, and in double quick time. Should your Ferret escape, there are a number of nasty and unpopular things which can happen, including the Ferret being savaged by dogs, run over by a vehicle, or caught eating your neighbour's prize Budgerigars, Goldfish and so on. You could loose friends very quickly with a Ferret on the loose, and it might not do the Ferret a lot of good either.

The Hutch

From an insecure hutch a Ferret will eventually gnaw and scratch a way out, especially if it is bored, gets little exercise or is being underfed. Thus, if you take a short cut in making a hutch, you could be in for a lot of problems. The illustration on the adjacent page will give a good idea of the sort of hutch needed for Ferrets: it is not a good idea to make it too small as this increases the risk of the animal fouling its body fur and bedding, and as already explained, this is one step away from a sick Ferret and two steps away from a dead one. Some of the larger pet shops, particularly those specialising in cage birds, will often

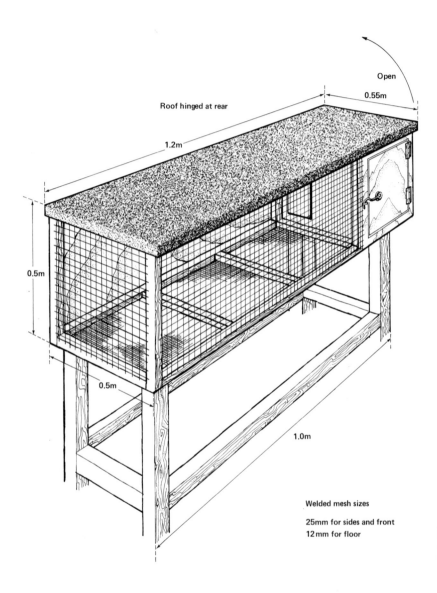

Open
0.55m
Roof hinged at rear
1.2m
0.5m
0.5m
1.0m

Welded mesh sizes

25mm for sides and front
12mm for floor

Fig. 4 Domestic Ferret hutch.

stock and sell welded wire mesh in various sizes. It is not cheap, but is by far the best and really the only satisfactory wire mesh. You cannot use rabbit or mouse netting as it is not strong enough and your Ferret will bite a hole through it in no time—in hours rather than days.

A wire mesh base is absolutely essential for the open run section, but not for the nest box area. This is another reason for using good, strong welded mesh as shown in Fig. 4, as it will support the weight of your Ferret without sagging. More importantly, it also allows the Ferret's scats or droppings to fall through and so keeps the hutch clean and healthy, which is vital. Locating your Ferret hutch in the right place is very important. If possible, it should be out of direct rainfall and even have a tar felt roof. It must not be situated where it is constantly buffeted by wind and most shady places could give suitable protection.

Another point of importance is if you have a good Ferret and the word gets around, then you may receive unwelcome visitors who would like to find out for themselves if the story is true and to relieve you of your Ferret! Try proving to a policeman that any particular Ferret is really yours; many before you have tried and failed. There is another good reason to keep your Ferret in a safe place and that is that an unhappily large number of people, often raised in towns and cities, have a very sick attitude to animals and will do the most utterly cruel things to any creature unlucky enough to cross their path.

Cleaning

Cleaning a Ferret hutch at regular intervals is always good policy and keeping it clean is quite easy with a wire mesh floor; it is easy for you and easy for the Ferret. Periodic disinfecting is essential and this needs to be fairly frequent in the summer months. As far as I am concerned, I like the smell of Ferrets and so may you and others you know. However, there are just as many, and maybe more who will object, particularly neighbours if you have them. One little trick is to put a wooden tray, such as you might get from a fruit shop, underneath the raised hutch directly below the area used for dropping the scats. If you fill this with dry earth or sawdust, or even cat litter, you can then easily remove the box, dispose of the droppings and any soiled litter, top up the box, rake it and then replace it. This all makes for a simple life and reduces the chance of complaint about your 'smelly Ferret'.

Bedding

Bedding in the nest box can be made up of a number of different things depending on what is easiest to obtain. Materials include dried peat moss from a garden centre, sawdust or wood shavings from a joiner's workshop (or sometimes you can get these shavings from a fruit shop as they are often used to pack soft fruit such as peaches or grapes), straw and hay are really the very best of nesting materials, but unless you live in a rural area these might not always be readily available. Another material, though possibly the least acceptable, is newspaper; five minutes tearing a newspaper to shreds will get you out of trouble until you can obtain better bedding material.

The ideal set up in a nest box is a layer of sawdust, wood chips or peat moss on the floor to the depth of a matchstick, and then loosely fill the rest of the nest box with hay, straw, or if you are stuck, newspaper shredded into thin strips. Ferrets do like to burrow into their bedding as it makes them feel secure and the fluffed-up bedding traps the warm air from their bodies and keeps them insulated in really cold weather. Sawdust or peat moss will insulate the Ferret from any draughts or damp from underneath and will also absorb any moisture from the fur, should it have been out working or exercising in the rain or damp grass.

The Ferret will not foul its bedding unless it is a sick animal and if the bedding has been fouled, then you have a very sick animal indeed; even when unwell, a Ferret will try to get over to its toilet. The Ferret scats should be firm and long in shape, about the thickness of a pencil. The colouring is not too important

Dog Ferret at entrance to his hutch. Notice ample clean bedding.

as it depends on what the animal has been eating. If, however, they are a sticky, shapeless mess then the animal has a problem with its stomach, perhaps from being fed either stale or rotten food, which leads me to the subject of feeding. If, as I say, the scats are a sticky mess it may be best to withdraw all food except for milk and bread for a day or two. Should things not get back to normal then contact your veterinary surgeon, tell him the position and ask his advice (see also Chapter 5).

Feeding

Feeding your Ferret can be rather bewildering to begin with if you have no previous experience. In addition, getting into the routine of obtaining sufficient food of the right kind can be very worrying. However, it all sorts itself out eventually and you will become used to feeding your animal.

As far as supplies are concerned, should you live in a large town or city, you will need to try and make a few friends in the right places. Do not waste time by going to supermarkets as their

Feeding bowl for Ferret. These vary but usually best made from metal to save breakages or swallowing pieces of plastic.

meat products are all pre-packed and usually not on the premises. A number of useful sources include the local butcher, especially if you already shop there; butchers are usually very obliging to their regular customers and may be willing to lay aside a few scraps at little or no cost (or possibly already produce a pet mince). If you are feeding raw meat, try not to let the Ferret eat too much fat as this binds them up inside, causing some discomfort; besides this, the food value of lumps of fat is not very high.

Do not, under any circumstances, feed pig meat in any form whatsoever. The risk of Salmonella infection is too great and this is of particular importance during the hot summer months; it is simply not worth the risk as only a tiny piece of meat can do all the damage.

Another source, and I believe the very best one, is the day-old chick culls from a poultry station or hatchery. The telephone directory will tell you if there is one of these in your area. I feed all our animals—Weasels, Polecats, Martens, Badgers, Foxes, Owls and birds of prey—on day-old chicks and some of these animals get nothing else. This diet provides a 'complete' food of protein, calcium, vitamins and roughage. Our Polecats and Ferrets are fed variously two or three chicks each per day, depending on the weather and how much exercise they have had. In cold weather or when out working, three chicks should be adequate, but in the summer they do not have the problem of heat loss that occurs in the winter months. Bitches do not necessarily eat less than dog Ferrets. However, when the bitch is pregnant or feeding and rearing young, she will definitely need more and as the youngsters grow, whatever you are feeding will need to be positively shovelled in. A growing Ferret eats and eats, and so do all its brothers and sisters.

A few words on the subject of what not to feed might be advisable at this stage, particularly in view of the fact that bad feeding is one of the most frequent abuses often unknowingly perpetrated on the Ferret. I am referring in particular to a main diet of bread and milk slops which is commonly given by some Ferret keepers. It bears no resemblance in the remotest way to the natural diet of an adult Ferret and it amazes me that people will even think of feeding it as a daily dose. The Ferret is a carnivore and like all carnivores it is broadly classed as a meat eater. Thus, to stay healthy, a Ferret must have meat—and not just occasionally, but every day. Without wishing to become too technical, the metabolism of any creature, from humans to mice is geared to a particular diet and sooner or later any major variation from the norm can (and often will) lead to problems with health. If you cannot or will not provide your Ferret with a proper diet, then you may well be safer collecting postage stamps as a pastime—the Ferret certainly will be.

Another policy of benefit to Ferrets and other carnivores is to feed six days out of seven, 'starving' the animal on the seventh day but always providing liquids. The reason for this practice is that carnivores in the wild do not naturally eat every day, but only as hunting success allows. Their bodies benefit from a 'food free' day now and again. Do not, however, take your Ferret hunting on one of these days, he will be keen you can be sure, but is quite likely to have a nice large meal down below ground and then snooze it off for a few hours!

[7]
Breeding

This is an interesting side of Ferret keeping, but it must be done with a purpose and not because it would be 'a nice thing to try'. Before even starting you must be sure that you are able to find any offspring a good home.

The Natural Cycle

If your Ferret is a female, it is in her interests to allow her to breed, if only once. This is true for all mammals, as without reproducing—which is, after all, what we are all here to do—there is a fairly high risk of internal problems with the animal's reproductive organs. In some species, including humans, these sensitive organs have to be removed by the operation known as a hysterectomy.

In the wild, Polecats pair up from March onwards, depending on which part of Europe they inhabit, as pairing becomes later the farther north one travels. This is due to a lengthening of the 'photo period', or increasing daylight after mid-winter; in the northernmost parts of the Polecat's range—Scotland, southern Sweden and Finland—this pairing for mating most often occurs in April. In captivity, the Ferret can come into season from mid or late February onwards, with the Steppe Polecat starting in early March.

Mating

The accurate indication of the commencement of your Ferrets

breeding season can be ascertained by checking the vulva of the female. When oestrous starts, the vulva will become swollen, protruding slightly, and about the size of a pea. Assuming you have access to a dog Ferret, this is the time he should be put in with the bitch. I feel it is better to put the dog with the bitch (and not the other way around) for this would put him on unfamiliar territory and might take a little of the edge off his aggression. Some dogs can be very harsh with their mates, particularly if the dog is a very big one and the bitch a very small one. The chief reason is that all members of the Mustelid family of animals, to which Ferrets, Polecats and Otters belong, share a common behaviour when coupling. This involves a great deal of preliminary noise as they chase around, and is followed by the dog seizing the bitch by the neck at the base of the skull when mounting her for copulation. He will hold her in this position for as much as an hour. Whatever you do, do not attempt to interfere in any way—all is well. It may seem rough, but without this aggression mating will not be successful, and whilst there is always the chance that the dog might kill the bitch—as can happen among the Mink kept on fur farms—it is a very rare occurrence. So take yourself off for a walk somewhere or put your feet up and have a cup of coffee; you are of no help and by staying could become a positive hindrance.

Pregnancy

When the Ferrets are moving around separately again, I would advise that the dog should be removed to a another hutch or cage and only brought back after at least one whole day. By this time the pair may well mate again, but equally likely, especially on the second day after mating, the dog may not be interested in the bitch. This will mean the first mating was successful, and if in one week's time you check the bitch again, you should find that her vulva is no longer swollen and is almost back to normal.

You must now wait for 41–42 days and it is a good idea to make a note in a diary or mark the days on a calendar. Do not work your bitch Ferret after 3–4 weeks of pregnancy. She will not be fit enough, and her reactions may be fractionally slower. In this condition, should she meet up with a big buck Rabbit who lands a kick on her side, then both she and her young ones may be injured.

Another thing to avoid is two females sharing a hutch when one or both have young. Unfortunately, they are not adverse to eating one another's offspring—a needless loss that could be avoided.

Try to avoid increasing the bitch's food supply too much during pregnancy, but make sure she has all she needs after parturition; it reduces the risk of cannibalism of her own young and ensures that they will grow satisfactorily.

Young

When the young are born they are blind, hairless and only weigh about 10g; there can be up to six in the litter. It is as well to avoid disturbing the nest of young unduly by opening it up to look inside, and under no circumstances touch the young until at least two weeks old; a nervous bitch may easily kill her young in a panic. Once the young are weaned, at about 8 weeks, they may be separated from their mother, but make sure first that you do actually see them eating. Remember also that they will need to be well fed both in quantity and in quality if you are not to produce a litter of runts.

It is well worth mentioning that however tame she ordinarily happens to be, a bitch Ferret will attack anyone going near her young often as not. It is as well to leave them alone; look and count if you can, but keep your fingers to yourself, or you may well learn what it feels like to be a Rabbit confronted with a Ferret!

Once the Ferrets have been weaned, and even for a week or two before that time, they will take up a great deal of your time as you must handle them as much as possible, feed them by hand, play with them, tickle them and fondle them. All this is essential to ensure you avoid producing a biter—and biting is a habit hard to break. Constant human contact with the young at this stage will make all the difference between a Ferret which is a pleasure to work with and one which is a constant nuisance.

[8]
Training

Obviously, before you go out ferreting you are going to need a Ferret! What to get and where to get it from is the point where you enter the realms of chance.

In theory, each and every Ferret should hunt Rabbits, but you do not want one that hunts Rabbits just any old way. The whole idea is to get it to hunt for you, and as effectively and efficiently as possible.

It is highly unlikely that anyone with a good working Ferret is going to be willing to sell it after it has been trained. Thus if you come across a good one for sale you have to ask yourself why? Because the seller is basically a generous person? Well, maybe, but then again ask yourself could it be that perhaps there just might be a little something wrong with the animal? Could there even be a great deal wrong with it?

If you take the risk of buying in these circumstances, then that is your privilege, but I would suggest that a better course would be to buy a young Ferret and let it grow up with you, learning your ways as you must learn his ways.

Animal Character

Every animal under the sun is different in its behaviour, and it is likely that there are as many nervous Ferrets as there are people who keep them. Therefore, if you get a highly-strung animal let us hope you yourself are placid, otherwise the pair of you are going to make a real mess of each other! A word often banded around is that old favourite 'vicious', as in 'that one was born vicious', and so on. Let me tell you an unpalatable secret: there is no such thing as a vicious animal. One may well meet animals who have been made vicious, most often by their ill treatment by humans. If you get bitten you will ask yourself the question 'what did I do wrong?'—because you or possibly somebody else before you must have done something to upset the animal. It is well worth remembering that the human race is the only animal walking the face of the earth that hunts and kills for pleasure. To illustrate this point, I am ready to wager that not one single person reading this book is so hungry that he hunts his Ferret for the pot and the pot alone. If anyone was so hungry I would guess that in most of what we know as the western world, they would have spent the price of this book to buy food instead. The brutal fact is that you want to hunt your Ferret for sport and that alone. However, a Rabbit for the table is always a welcome thing. If you can face up to that fact and that you are asking your Ferret to help you, then remember that it is very easy for the Ferret to misunderstand your actions and react in defence, sometimes by biting. It is thus necessary to avoid this possibility by constant handling, so that the Ferret comes to trust you completely. Look at it this way; you are a team, you are no good without the animal, but without you it could go its own way quite happily. So if you stick your hand into a hole or bag, it is re-assuring to know that the Ferret will not bite you if it has nothing to fear, real or imagined. Likewise, suppose you are a Ferret and see a huge hand that sometimes hurts you when it picks you up; then the temptation to bite in defence will be pretty strong. The animal bites because it is frightened of you; what other reason is more obvious?

Sources of Ferrets

Where does one obtain a Ferret? There are a number of possibilities, a small advertisement in the local newspaper or the farming press—or for the U.K. in *Exchange & Mart*, a weekly 'sell everything' paper. The best time is late summer or early

Carrying box, showing simple design and general size for one ferret.

autumn, but kits born in April can be obtained from June onwards. Once independent of their mother and eating lustily, they will be ready to grace the quarters you have constructed for them. Pick a 'bouncer', something full of energy; pick it up and fluff up the fur to see if there are any inflamed patches of skin. If there are, do not, whatever you do take it from that owner— move on! There will be plenty more to choose from, so do not worry and play it safe.

Training Practice

Let us assume you have acquired a young Ferret and have been handling it constantly, lifting it in and out of its hutch, tickling it, exercising it, playing with it and feeding it. What you must be aiming to achieve is getting that little Ferret to grow up thinking of your hands as being the next best thing to Santa Claus in the land of Ferrets. You must make that Ferret fall head over heels in love with your fingers; it has got to be so fond of them that you dare not even take them out of your pockets. Seriously, if the Ferret thinks of your hands as being associated with happy events, there is little chance that it will bite.

Having avoided teaching your animal to bite, the next thing you want to avoid it knowing is that it is going to be pounced on, scooped up and frightened half to death every time it shows its face out of a burrow. Unless you exercise restraint when lifting up your Ferret, it is going to develop an aversion to coming out of any burrow after clearing out the Rabbits for you. Let it come out and poke around, then quietly walk over and tickle or stroke it; then pick it up.

Carrying Ferrets

Another good trick to bear in mind is that no creature, either human or Ferret, likes to be shut up in the dark in a strange place. Thus before you ever take your Ferret out on its first

Removing Ferret. Note careful but firm grip as animal
is lifted out.

expedition, let it familiarise itself with the travelling bag or box. A good idea is to put an old towel beside the bedding in the nest box of the hutch for a few days so the Ferret's scent can be transferred to it. Take this towel out and place it in the travelling bag or box, and always keep it there. Do not use the container for any other purpose at all. For a few days lift the Ferret out of the hutch and let it play in and out and around the bag or box; it will explore it thoroughly. Try this a few times and the container will be so familiar to the Ferret, scent and all, that it will hold no terrors for the animal and it will probably travel quite happily with you, probably snoozing and dreaming about giant buck Rabbits!

Whether you use a bag or a box, it must be well ventilated with small holes punched or drilled at regular intervals all around the top. A half-cooked Ferret is not going to catch very much, that is certain. The ideal sort of bag is the pliable type with a shoulder strap, sometimes seen endorsed with the name of an airline or sports goods manufacturer upon it. It does not need to be big, but it must be escape-proof, and having a zipper type opening does help a great deal—and remember, getting in and out of tight corners is part of a Ferret's professional expertise!

[9]
Hunting with Ferrets

Never hunt in the summertime—and never means *never*, for several good reasons. Firstly, the Rabbits will most probably have young and the doe is quite likely to put up a spirited defence of the little ones. Should she land a kick in the ribs of your Ferret, especially if it is the smaller bitch Ferret, then you can hardly blame her if she refuses to go down again; and remember, Rabbits can bite too. Secondly, if the doe does bolt out leaving her kits to the Ferret, it is almost certain that the Ferret is going to have a very pleasant and large meal. After such a large meal, calmly eaten as you become more and more frustrated above ground, the Ferret will in all probability settle down to sleep—possibly for hours and hours. Meanwhile, up above, on a blazing hot day, what are you going to do? You cannot go and leave the Ferret, so you have either to sit and wait, or start digging with no certainty of arriving at the precise spot where your Ferret is dozing. Digging in any weather is hot work, but digging in hot summer sunshine is murder!

Another point to consider is that if you kill off the youngsters in the nest, what do you hunt next year?

Hunting in Winter

Most sensible people Rabbit in the winter months. There is then no heavy undergrowth to make netting difficult or to restrict vision. It always seems to be the hole you fail to cover with the net that Rabbits use for an exit.

The morning following a good fall of snow is a very useful time to find which holes have residents. Rabbit tracks are always in pairs as a result of the way they walk. Watch out though for smaller tracks which might mean you have Rats at home; be very careful! Of course, it could also be that the smaller cousins of the Ferrets—Stoats or Weasels—have been calling. You are not the only one with the bright idea of hunting, and they are doing it to survive. Snow can certainly provide you with a great deal of information if you know how to 'read' it. However, without snow all is not so obvious, but there are plenty of points to look for; pea-size black droppings at the mouth of the hole means 'occupied' most of the time, as does bare earth around the entrance. If the entrance has a covering of leaves, then this more than likely means 'unoccupied'—but beware as it could be that all it means is that this entrance is one of several to an underground tunnel system and is not favoured as a route. It will need to be netted, just in case.

Ready to Hunt

Assuming you have a manageable Ferret, access to Rabbit country and the means to get yourself and your Ferret safely there, it should be possible to have an enjoyable day's hunting. Even if you catch little or nothing, there is a great deal to be seen and learnt in the countryside with the passing seasons. If nothing else, you and your Ferret will end up well exercised and so too might be the Rabbits, if you don't get your netting properly sorted out.

Hunting Teams

You can hunt Rabbits with just the Ferret and yourself; you can add a Terrier to the team; and you can also utilize one or more shotguns. In this case you can operate largely without nets, although it is always worth while taking them along just in case they are needed. These are the methods by which you can undertake

Ferret being removed from carrying box ready for hunting.

the job. all things being equal. However, all things are rarely equal. For example in the U.K. the user of a shotgun must first have a licence issued by the police. Secondly, it is vital that one knows how to use such a gun. Shooting your fellow hunters, or even the Ferret, from the spread of the shot is a good way to ruin the whole afternoon's hunting, not to mention the injury caused to whoever does get shot. So other than mentioning it as one of the methods, we will leave aside the shotgun and consider the other two methods together.

Nets

Have Ferret, will Rabbit! Well not quite, you will need nets and not just one or two, but several. It defeats the whole object of the enterprise to net five of the six holes and merely hope that the Rabbit will not use that unplugged one. Having obtained a good number of nets, and the best ones to use are those made for the purpose by a number of small manufacturing companies, you will have found that the cost is not so great. There is little point in making your own; it could mean watching with frustration as the biggest Rabbit you ever saw gets away. Fishermen have no monopoly on tall stories about 'the one that got away' you know.

Dogs

If you are very lucky you may come across a dog, probably a Terrier, but it could be any breed. If it is any good, it will mark an occupied hole in one of two ways. Firstly, it may make a lot of noise, yelping and scratching away at the hole. In this case don't invite him out on your next trip, as you can be sure that if you can hear him, then so can the Rabbit, who will then take immediate steps to get out and away. On the other hand, if the dog marks the hole by looking at it, wagging his tail and will not come off when called, then there is a good chance that he knows something you do not. What he will be trying to tell you is that

[56]

Albino Ferret working with a Pointer. Unfortunately this particular
dog's speciality is the vole.

he will keep an eye on this particular exit, while you quickly and
quietly run along and net up all the others before sending the
Ferret down to play war games.

Inexperienced Ferrets

There is an important point worth remembering when starting
to work an inexperienced Ferret, and that is that young Polecats
learn to hunt by example from their mothers. While you might
be lucky enough to get results first time out, it is by no means
certain, and do not be surprised if it takes half a dozen trips before
the Ferret catches on. However, when it does you are reasonably
assured your Ferret can be trusted not to forget. A practical way
to start is to feed the Ferret on Rabbit before starting to hunt.
This is a way of associating Rabbit smell with food from the
beginning and after this stage it is obviously not necessary.

[57]

Myxomatosis

Without fear of contradiction it is fair to state that the greatest influence on Rabbits, and hence upon ferreting has been myxomatosis and it seems likely to remain so. A little history and background to the disease is worth recording, as there is a great deal of nonsense spoken and written about it, mainly as a result of ignorance about the disease.

To begin with, myxomatosis originally came from South America. It was found that a native species of rodent, somewhat like the Rabbit, rarely died from the disease, but Rabbits from Europe certainly did. When this information became known, the owner of a property in France, which was virtually over-run with Rabbits, introduced the virus to his local population to see if it would have any effect as a control measure. It had a tremendous effect upon the Rabbits. In no time at all their numbers were greatly reduced and the disease covered a wide, and ever increasingly wider, area. On it raged through all of France, Belgium, Netherlands, Germany—in fact everywhere Rabbits were to be found. Without human assistance it would probably never have crossed the Channel, but cross it it did, either by the virus being injected, or, equally likely, by sick Rabbits being brought over to Britain. By 1953 much of England and Wales were affected and it had by then crossed the border into Scotland; the Rabbit suffered everywhere.

Almost overnight it seemed, farmers and foresters found themselves saving millions of pounds in protective measures and increased production. One figure I have seen quoted was £19 million for farmers and £15 million for foresters at mid-1950 prices, which in the late 1970's must be equal to several hundred millions of pounds.

Few people wept for the Rabbit, but myxomatosis remains a truly diabolical disease for any creature to suffer. Fortunately, it is not transmitted to any other animal, though, but it is thought that Hares may contract it on rare occasions.

Every disease originating from a virus is a living organism, and it is a common feature for those who suffer from the disease to develop an immunity, should they survive. This is equally true for the common cold and for myxomatosis. Now, if everyone develops immunity to a virus then surely that virus should become extinct. Unfortunately this is not so! Evolution has 'taught' all creatures to develop and strains of the virus adapt to changing conditions. In a large warren of Rabbits this meant that myxomatosis virus number 1 kills off 90% of the population, but leaves 10% to recover from the disease. This remaining 10% start to breed, their offspring passing on the immunity and in a few years the Rabbits are back to strength. There you are, happily ferreting away again, when suddenly along comes a new strain of the disease and you are out of work again. The whole story starts all over again with Rabbit numbers going up and down on a fairly regular cycle.

How do Rabbits catch myxomatosis? Well, it is that old eternal triangle again. First you have the host, who is the Rabbit; secondly, there is the disease, and thirdly you need a vector or agent and this is an insect—often a flea but sometimes a mosquito. You rarely see myxomatosis around in the winter. Insects do not reproduce at that time of the year, except in southern Europe. In a confined space, for example in the warren, the doe produces her young as the weather becomes warmer, but so does the flea. Along comes a Rabbit immune to the disease, but perhaps having flea eggs in its fur; it mates with the doe, some of the eggs fall off into her fur, lie there and eventually hatch. The young fleas bite the host Rabbit to suck its blood, passing the disease into the blood stream. From there on it is passed to the young Rabbits and is eventually passed on to the rest of the colony. Before long mid-summer arrives and there are dead and dying Rabbits everywhere.

For the ferreter there is a further important point about myxomatosis and some Rabbits in addition to the features mentioned above. In certain places, their behaviour, including reproduction, has been altered in a way which could affect ferreting. Certain populations of Rabbits have taken to living above ground, rather like Hares, and even produce their young in Hare-like forms in the vegetation. Obviously, ferreting these animals is well nigh impossible and one is tempted to say bring back the old-fashioned Rabbit!

Whilst there is no clinical reason why the flesh of a Rabbit with this disease should be inedible—it is really a psychological block—I must admit I would not be very enthusiastic about eating it myself. However, provided the head is lopped off and discarded, there is no reason why the meat should not be fed to the Ferrets or other animals. A word of caution; do not take the Rabbit home with its pelt still on as that would be a most blameworthy act. Skin it right away because the fleas in the fur could easily find their way on to a pet Rabbit nearby. Incidentally, it is possible to inoculate a Rabbit against the disease, and if you keep Rabbits and Ferret them in the wild, you ought to take that precaution. It would be very easy for fleas to lodge temporarily on your clothes or Ferret's fur and then hop across to the Rabbit hutch.

Out Hunting

Getting back to the actual job of ferreting, an inexperienced animal such as your youngster will be, needs indulging in the manner described earlier. His nose is his great asset and if he seems to dally around sniffing and only slowly entering the burrow, then let him; who is in a hurry anyway? Time is of no interest to the Ferret as measurement in minutes and hours is an exclusively human foible. Just sit down and watch. In time the Ferret disappears down into the hole quickly enough and if you are lucky you will have nets bulging all over the place. It is equally possible, of course, that you might not get quite this result, but it is always best to think positively.

Let us hope that if your Ferret meets a Rabbit that the Rabbit will decide to leave in a hurry, straight for your nets. The other possibilities are not so good; either the Rabbit will 'block'—that is, to face away from the Ferret, exposing its backside which will be bitten, scratched and otherwise abused by the Ferret who will eventually leave in disgust or, alternatively, the Ferret may kill

Ferret being carried by handler. Constant wriggling can lead to
many wrist scratches by those sharp little claws.

underground, and that can be a nuisance, especially if it starts to have a good meal then sleeps. If you are learning the trade, you can either wait or dig, assuming of course you brought a spade. However, if you have been at the game for some time and go out regularly, you may well have a large dog Ferret noted for its lack of personal charm. It is at this point that he is brought into the game as around his neck you will have most likely have fitted a little collar to which you can clip a line or a leash. Having done this, you put him down the hole and the theory is that he will find your other, more demure Ferret, and the Rabbit. He should then proceed to make strenuous efforts to claim the Rabbit for himself while making it very plain to the other Ferret that it should get off about its business. A useful tip is to put a knot in the line, usually a stout twine, every 30cm or so. As long as you know the distance between each knot and if they are evenly spaced, this will give you a guide as to know how far the animal has gone before you try to dig him out. However, one slight problem is that Rabbits do not dig in straight lines; they go along, around, up, down and back again.

Prevention is better than cure and you can muzzle the Ferret, which, incidentally they do not take to too well as it is most undignified and cramps their style. Alternatively, of course, an animal which is not hungry is less inclined to eat, so perhaps a small 'aperitif' before going out will avoid the problem of a Ferret eating while on the job. I am sure you would not be very keen to go out to work on an empty stomach, and neither is the Ferret.

A word of warning; lining a Ferret can be very dangerous for the animal. More Ferrets have become tangled up on rocks or tree roots and starved or strangled to death than I will ever have hot lunches. If you do fit a line, then do it thoroughly and if you find the animal is well and truly lost, get help to gass the burrow and put the Ferret to sleep painlessly. It is only the most callous and unfeeling humans who walk off and leave an animal to die, especially when the animal is a working partner.

Another word of warning; earlier I referred to the possibility of your Ferret receiving from a Rabbit a kick which can inflict serious injury. Remember that when you come to untangle a

Lined Ferret returning safely. Care must be exercised in lining to avoid animals being caught up in roots or rocks underground.

Rabbit which has bolted into a net, it only needs half a chance and it will be out and off. Given another half a chance and it will rake your skin with a hefty kick, and if you are bare armed and the toe nails connect, then you will be far from happy with the resulting scratches. Get your hands on to the back legs, hold them firmly (and I mean firmly because that Rabbit is going to be very angry), lift it up, net and all if you have to, and give it a sharp bang on the back of the head behind the ears using a thick stick or something similar. Then put it into a sack and check other nets. You may well have to work fast because a well populated warren will mean you could have Rabbits rushing around all over the place. Then there is always a very good chance that if one Rabbit hits a particular net, so will another, indicating a favourite exit for the burrow.

Ferret being returned to carrying or travelling box after being out and 'on a job'.

Successful Rabbiting

The measure of your success when ferreting is not just dependent on the keenness of the Ferret. It is not much good having a brilliant Ferret if you have made a poor job of the positioning and securing of the nets. A bolting Rabbit moves at quite a speed in an effort to escape certain death, and the idea is for it to hit the net and become irretrievably tangled. The net must stay in position, otherwise the Rabbit will be just a grey streak in your memory.

It is worth commenting that the ratio of success is proportionately less with the increase in numbers of people out in a group. One, two, perhaps even three of you and that is quite enough. Ferreting is not an occasion for a family outing and apart from anything else, a farmer seeing several households of people on his land is not going to be at all amused, nor will he be if you take along a dog who is likely to exercise the livestock.

*   *   *

Of course, there are other places to go ferreting; old quarries or council refuse tips, although you are more likely to turn up Rats there. If you want to ferret for Rats, then go right ahead. Personally, I think it is a crazy thing to do and I have nothing to offer in the way of advice, except don't!

[10]

Electronic Ferret Locators

In all likelihood, this must rank as the first real inovation in ferreting since Ferrets were first used to hunt. Science seems to catch up with everything and now, in theory at least, there is no reason to lose a Ferret ever again.

There are two basic systems which seem to have been developed by users of locators. One of these is to fit a Ferret with a locator every time one is out working. The other method is to operate your Ferret as per normal, but when your animal lies up, instead of lining another Ferret, send down a Ferret fitted with a locator. Then, having pin-pointed the position of the original animal, just start digging if the first Ferret has not already been flushed out by the second.

In short, no matter how twisted or complicated might be the system of runs, you can identify with complete accuracy just exactly where your Ferret is lying and dig straight down to retrieve it.

There are two positions for the collar-mounted transmitter, either on the top behind the ears, or underneath around the throat. The latter position seems to be the best as it avoids snagging on branching roots underground, or where a tunnel narrows and blocks the Ferret. Either way, the animal can become caught up, which means an unpleasant dig. I would certainly favour the throat position to avoid this possibility. Also, guard against choking the animal as a result of fitting the collar too tightly.

Technical Details

The weight of the locator is minimal and is hardly likely to be noticed once the Ferret has become used to wearing it. Mounted in an epoxy resin case, the long-wave transmitter is able to withstand shock damage. This case also contains the 'hearing aid' size battery as power source and is fitted to a very soft leather strap with adjustable buckle suitable for both dog and bitch Ferrets.

The radio signal from the collar is picked up by a hand-held transistorised receiver, either in a case or in the form of a scanner rod with handgrip. There is also an earphone which is needed for use with the scanner rod but is optional for the case. The equipment is supplied with either system.

Operation of the Locator

For obvious reasons the batteries have to be new and with polarity correctly positioned. Before going out working it is essential to tune the receiver correctly. This must be done out of doors as the electrical circuit in the house will cause interference. Being a directional signal, it is very important to remember while you get a strong signal in one direction, reception at right angles will be quite weak. It is worthwhile carrying spare batteries each for the receiver and transmitter.

The manufacturers claim a minimum range of 6 feet (1·9m) and an average of 8 feet (2·4m) and it is unlikely that Rabbits will dig deeper than that, if they do they are either mad or will scare your Ferret to death.

One interesting advantage of this equipment is that if used in conjunction with a shotgun, some unfair advantages can be had over the Rabbit. By using the scanner, the progress of the Ferret can be followed and wherever he goes, all Rabbits are likely to go before. Thus it is easy to anticipate the direction they are likely to take. However, please do not shoot the Ferret as they all emerge together!

[68]

It is very important to keep the receiver and transmitting locator dry when out working. When the Ferret is underground, the transmitter will obviously be protected from the rain, but it needs to be carefully checked and cleaned, especially the battery. The receiver is more prone to being rain damaged or could even be dropped in a puddle! It should be carried in a transparent polythene bag which enables you to see the controls and keeps it dry. This will not reduce the signal strength in any way but will save the circuit from corrosion.

The signal is a 'tat-tat-tat' bleep which becomes louder as the user draws closer to the locator fitted to the Ferret. Walk slowly across the warren, sweeping the receiver slowly back and forth until the signal is picked up with the receiver at maximum volume. Then 'home in' on the signal by reducing the volume as low as possible until you can just hear the bleep. You are, at that point, closest to your Ferret and if you need to dig, then you are at the right spot.

Ferret locator with handset on the right, ear-plugs below; collar on the left, fitted with small transmitter.

Albino Ferret alert and listening, hoping to catch a scent on the wind.

Difficulties

Because this equipment works on a radio frequency, you are unlikely to encounter any problems over the signal strength caused by underground rocks. However, if the signal is weak it could be for one of two reasons: one or both pieces of equipment may have weak batteries, or alternatively, you may have failed to tune the receiver properly and the Ferret, wearing its locator, is at the limit or out of range entirely. If there is a problem it is most likely to be caused by misuse rather than by a fault with the equipment. It is, after all, very simple to use and is based upon the sample principle as a transistor radio. Either it works or it does not, and if it only works badly then you are to blame as likely as not.

It is neither desirable nor possible to have a greater range than is available; the range is very workable and any greater range could cause conflict with the broadcasting authorities, a point to bear in mind for those of you who are electronics enthusiasts; do not be tempted to make any modifications.

Conclusions

Personally, I think this is a very neat and useful piece of equipment for Ferreting and should save the lives of Ferrets lost underground which would not previously have been located despite extensive digging. The cost is amazingly low and the advantages are very considerable.

[11]
Conclusion

It is never easy to be completely objective and to give the best advice. However, I do have a long standing interest in all members of the Mustelid family, to which the Ferret belongs, and at one time or another I have kept most of the species—except the Wolverine, and some day I may be lucky with that one. Thus, I have had much relevant experience on which to base my views. I have also collected together a fairly extensive list of publications, mainly of a scientific nature, from which I have learnt a great deal and upon which I base much that is offered in this small book.

This book is not intended as the last word on Ferrets and their use, but should best be thought of as an introduction to the subject, which the reader can then take further or leave alone as he feels inclined.

Should you decide to pursue ferreting seriously, please remember that almost without fail you will have to go on to land owned by someone else, and in some parts of the world the Rabbits are the property of the owner. Also, wherever you are it pays handsomely to obtain the landowner's approval, which will often be granted and may even lead to active help and encouragement of your aims. If he says 'no', as he has a perfect right to do, thank him for his time and ask elsewhere. It could be that he might change his mind if he then learns from the neighbouring land owner that you are a careful and obliging person.

There are other important points to bear in mind. The most usual time to ferret is during the winter months and some farms rent out the shooting rights of the land as part of their livelihood.

Thus if you work an area shortly before a shoot is due to take place, you may find yourself to be very unpopular indeed; and you may lose a good territory. Remember that the land you cross for pleasure is worked for a living by someone else. You can learn a good deal of natural history from a book, but the field craft only comes from experience, and if you can find a helpful and friendly gamekeeper or countryman who will take you in tow and give you that practical experience, then you will improve by leaps and bounds.

When all is said and done, however, the most important thing about ferreting is the Ferret. Without a good one you are lost, and they are all basically good to begin with: from the very beginning it is the way in which you handle them that counts. Properly fed and properly handled, treated from the outset with kindness and respect, you can have a good partner.

Albino Ferret clearly showing the humped back, characteristic of all the mustelid family, including stoats, badgers and otters.

Glossary of Terms

ALBINO   An animal without colour pigment in its fur, giving a white coat and pink eyes; inbreeding among Ferrets is the common cause.

BITCH FERRET   The female Ferret; also sometimes referred to as a Jill.

BLOCKED   A Rabbit which has stopped in a tunnel or dead end and faces away from the Ferret, preventing it from passing.

COPULATION   The mating act between the male and female of any species.

COUPLING   See COPULATION.

DOG FERRET   The male Ferret, also sometimes referred to as a Hob.

FERRET   A domesticated Polecat descended from the Steppe Polecat and used for hunting. They are either albino or with Polecat-type markings. Known scientifically as *Mustela eversmani furo*.

HUTCH   A cage or kennel for keeping FERRETS.

INBREEDING   The mating of closely related animals, e.g. brother to sister, mother to son, etc.

LINE   A long leash used while running some Ferrets underground.

OESTROUS   The heat period, or reproductive condition.

PARTURITION   The act of giving birth to the young.

PENIS   The male reproductive organ.

POLECAT   A free living wild Mustelid, either of the European or Steppe species, which are known, respectively, as *Mustela putorious* or *Mustela eversmanni*.

RUNT   An animal which is either unusually small at birth or which fails to grow to a proper size due to poor feeding or inbreeding.

SCATS   Sometimes referred to as droppings, dung, stools or faeces.

VULVA   The outer feature of the female reproductive organ.

WEANING   The age at which a young animal is independent of its mother and can be safely removed.

WELDED MESH   Wire mesh, either square or oblong openings made from strong gauge galvanised wire.

Suppliers' Addresses *

Abbot Bros, Thuxton, Norfolk.
Bryants, 16 Ditton Hill Road, Long Ditton, Surrey.
K. P. & S. Nets, 80 Hermitage Street, Crewkerne, Somerset.
Gallimore, 10 Winterborne Monkton, Dorchester, Dorset.

*The above are suppliers of Ferrets, Nets and other items for Ferreting in the U.K. and can be contacted for their lists of available products and current prices. Similar suppliers exist in North America and elsewhere and their addresses can usually be obtained from the appropriate field sport magazines, ferreting enthusiasts, etc.

Index